My Capital

J. Jean Robertson

ROURKE PUBLISHING

www.rourkepublishing.com

www.rourkepublishing.com

PHOTO CREDITS: Cover: © Matthew Carrol; Title Page: © Noclip; Page 3: © csreed; Page 5: © LyaC; Page 7: © AP Images; Page 9, 19: © Olga Bogatyrenko; Page: 11: © mikadx; Page 13: © Gary Blakeley; Page 14: © lolie; Page 15: ©RobertDodge; Page 16: © nojustice; Page 17: © jmaehl; Page 20: © narvikk, © sjlocke; Page 21: © National Park Service, Harpers Ferry Center; Page 22: © jmaehl, © Gary Blakeley, © csreed; Page 23: © Olga Bogatyrenko, © LyaC

E;dited by Meg Greve

Cover design by Renee Brady
Interior design by Renee Brady

Library of Congress Cataloging-in-Publication Data

Robertson, J. Jean.
 My capital / J. Jean Robertson.
    p. cm. -- (Little world social studies)
 Includes bibliographical references and index.
 ISBN 978-1-61590-331-3 (Hard Cover) (alk. paper)
 ISBN 978-1-61590-570-6 (Soft Cover)
 1. Washington (D.C.)--Juvenile literature. I. Title.
 F194.3.R63 2011
 975.3--dc22
                                   2010009261

Rourke Publishing
Printed in the United States of America, North Mankato, Minnesota
033010
033010LP

www.rourkepublishing.com - rourke@rourkepublishing.com
Post Office Box 643328 Vero Beach, Florida 32964

Let's take a ride around the capital of the United States, Washington, D.C. We'll take the **Metro**!

Many government buildings are in D.C. and many people work in these buildings to keep my country running.

Capital Fact

D.C. is short for District of Columbia.

Every U.S. president except the first, George Washington, has lived and worked in the White House.

Capital Fact

The current president, Barack Obama, lives in the White House with his family, Michelle, Malia, Sasha, and their dog named Bo.

The Capitol Building is the place where **senators** and **representatives** from all fifty states meet to make laws for our country.

The Pentagon is a huge, five-sided building. People work there to keep my country safe.

Capital Fact

The Pentagon is the largest office building in the world.

Many **memorials** and monuments are in D.C. Some are in Arlington National Cemetery.

Capital Fact

The Marine Corps War Memorial shows five marines and one sailor raising a U.S. flag on Iwo Jima.

Others are part of the National Mall.

Vietnam Veteran's Memorial
The Three Soldiers

World War II Memorial

15

The Lincoln Memorial honors Abraham Lincoln, my country's sixteenth president.

A peaceful place in my capital is the National **Cathedral**.

My capital also has museums. The **Smithsonian Institution** includes 19 museums, 9 research centers, and a zoo!

There's so much to see and do in my capital. Let's go!

capital Fact

It costs to ride the Metro trains, but visiting all the special places is free!

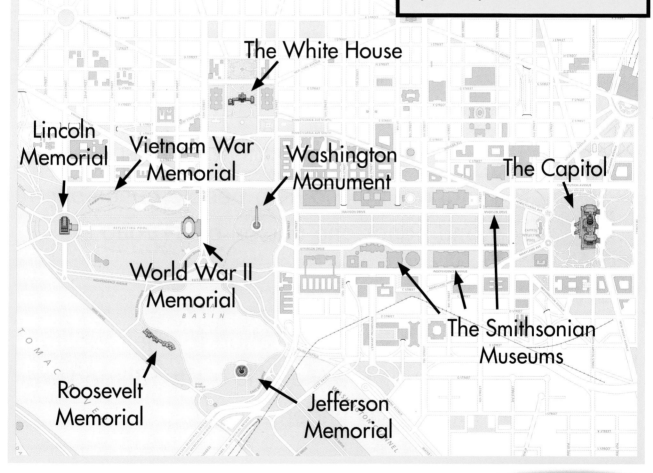

The White House

Lincoln Memorial

Vietnam War Memorial

Washington Monument

The Capitol

World War II Memorial

The Smithsonian Museums

Roosevelt Memorial

Jefferson Memorial

Picture Glossary

cathedral (kuh-THEE-druhl): A large, important church.

memorials (muh-MOR-ee-uhlz): Places that are built to help people remember and honor one person or a group of people.

Metro (MET-roh): Short for metropolitan railroad. The Metro is a city railroad which runs mostly underground.

representatives (rep-ri-ZEN-tuh-tivs): People elected every two years by each state to help make the laws of the country.

senators (SEN-it-ers): People elected every six years by each state to help make the laws of our country. There are two senators for each state.

Smithsonian Institution (smith-SO-nee-uhn in-sti-TOO-shuhn): A museum named for James Smithson who gave all of his wealth to create a place of learning.

Index

Websites

www.fbi.gov/fbikids

www.stamps.org/KIDS

www.smithsonianeducation.org/students

www.usmint.gov/kids

About the Author

J. Jean Robertson, also known as Bushka to her grandchildren and many other kids, loves to read, travel, and write books for children. After teaching for many years, she retired to San Antonio, Florida, where she lives with her husband.

mL

12/10